Contents

Preface

The topic of the end times has always interested Christians. What does the Bible teach about judgment day and the events leading up to it? Does the Bible give us certain signs to look for, warning us that the end is near? Are specific current events prophesied in Scripture? The Bible has much to teach us on this topic.

At the same time, many false teachings have arisen over the years, teachings about the millennium, the rapture, the great tribulation, and attempts to set dates for end-time events. Books such as *The Late Great Planet Earth* and the currently popular Left Behind series have sold millions of copies and have even been made into full-length movies. What does the Bible say about such teachings? What can we know for sure about the end times?

This little booklet, written by Pastor Harold Wicke and originally published as a series of articles in the *Northwestern Lutheran,* addresses these questions. Pastor Wicke's answers from Scripture are as timely today as when he first wrote them a generation ago. He discusses many of the ever-present false teachings concerning the end times, and more importantly, he lets Scripture speak for itself concerning the end times. Most important, Pastor Wicke shows how what the Bible teaches concerning the end times serves the gospel and is meant to comfort and encourage Christians as they live their faith, ever waiting for the Lord to return on the Last Day.

We are pleased to offer this booklet to a new generation of God's people who eagerly long for the Lord's appearing.

The Publisher

I

The Millennium— Is It Christian?

What will it be like before the end of the world? This is how it has been described:

At the close of this present age, there will come a happy period, the days of the Messiah. Ransomed Israel will be miraculously gathered from the ends of the earth and brought back to their own land. The dead too will be raised. All resistance to God will be concentrated in a great war that will bring dreadful suffering to Israel. Three times the enemy will storm the Holy City, but each time the assault will be repelled. At last the enemy will be completely destroyed. Jerusalem will then become the dwelling place of Israel, and all nations will resort to it. The new temple that the Messiah will rear will be more glorious than ever. The land will spontaneously produce the finest crops; every tree will become a fruit-bearer. All sickness and disease, and all that can hurt, will cease. Life will be greatly prolonged. Jerusalem will, as

> the residence of the Messiah, become the capital of the world, and Israel will take the place of the world powers. When the nations, who have hitherto given tribute to the Messiah, later rebel against him, he will utterly destroy them by the breath of his mouth. Then the final judgment will commence.

Who wrote that? Does the above sound as though it were a quotation from Hal Lindsey's book *The Late Great Planet Earth*? He does say many of the same things; but the above is actually an abbreviated summary of what the ancient rabbis were teaching already before the days of Jesus Christ. So these thoughts are not Christian at all. They are an expression of Jewish hopes and speculations in a time of oppression. But they are an accurate picture of what Israel expected its Messiah to accomplish.

Christ in action

Compare the previous description with what Jesus said in the gospels about his kingdom, the end of the world, and his coming again, and you can see why the people of his day were disappointed in him. He wasn't what their teachers had led them to expect with their fantastic misinterpretations of Scripture.

Jesus, as we know, spoke not of an earthly kingdom but of his coming again, of the final judgment, and of eternity. He warned those who opposed him: "As the Father has life in himself, so he has granted the Son to have life in himself. . . . And he has given him authority to judge because he is the Son of Man" (John 5:26,27). To the high priest and the members of the Sanhedrin who condemned him, he said, "In the future you will see the Son of Man sitting at the right hand of the Mighty One and coming on the clouds of heaven" (Matthew 26:64). That, not a millennium, was the future they faced.

That the Lord's disciples, as they grew up, were also exposed to these ideas is evident from the gospels. Recall that Peter didn't want to hear about any suffering and dying on the part of Jesus. The Lord had to remind him and the others, "The Son of Man is going to come in his Father's glory with his angels, and then he will reward each person according to what he has done" (Matthew 16:27). The final echo came shortly before Jesus' ascension, when the disciples asked, "Lord, are you at this time going to restore the kingdom to Israel?" (Acts 1:6). After Pentecost the Holy Spirit cleansed their teaching of all such false hopes.

A carryover

False hopes have a way of not dying out very fast. Thus, it's not surprising that some of the early teachers in the church, after the days of the apostles, fell for these rabbinical teachings again. After all, everyone would like to have heaven on earth. However, when the church later formulated its confessions of faith, all such nonbiblical teachings were rigorously excluded.

The creeds

The earliest form of the Apostles' Creed dates back to about A.D. 150. It received its final form in the fifth century. There isn't the faintest whisper about a millennium in this creed. It states straightforward: "From there he will come to judge the living and the dead." Christ's second coming coincides with the final judgment.

The Nicene Creed of A.D. 325 says this about our Lord: "He will come again in glory to judge the living and the dead, and his kingdom will have no end. . . . We look for the resurrection of the dead and the life of the world to come." Again, no millennium!

The Athanasian Creed echoes the words of Jesus himself as found in Matthew 25. After confessing the doctrines of the Trinity, the divinity of Christ, and the redemption through Christ, it states, "He [Christ] . . . is seated at the right hand of God the Father almighty, and from there will come to judge the living and the dead. At his coming all people will rise with their own bodies to answer for their personal deeds. Those who have done good will enter eternal life, but those who have done evil will go into eternal fire." No room for a millennium!

The Augsburg Confession

Many years later the Lutheran church in Article XVII of the Augsburg Confession took the same stand: "Also they teach that at the consummation of the world Christ will appear for judgment, and will raise up all the dead; He will give to the godly and elect eternal life and everlasting joys, but ungodly men and the devils He will condemn to be tormented without end. . . . They condemn also others, who are now spreading certain Jewish opinions, that before the resurrection of the dead the godly shall take possession of the kingdom of the world, the ungodly being everywhere suppressed."

The confessions of the Lutheran church want nothing to do with any such millennial opinions or any variations of them. They recognize that such opinions are not Christian—not taught by Christ.

Of course, the creeds are not the final authority, and lest anyone suggest that we are setting the creeds above Scripture, we will turn to Scripture in the next chapter and ask, What kind of a kingdom did our Lord come to establish? Is it in existence now, or is it dated sometime in the future? In other words, was Christ a millennialist? The answer, of course, is no. But I'm sure you will want to see the evidence.

II

Is Christ's Kingdom Millennial?

If things have been going all wrong, if life hardly seems worth living, if evil seems to prevail at times—even in the courts—and you are wondering how much longer the Lord can put up with man's sinfulness, then (according to Billy Graham's book *World Aflame,* page 195) you may nevertheless take heart, because "the Christian has tomorrow. It is the Kingdom of God on earth."

Strange, but that isn't the hope that is being offered us in our churches. Are we possibly being misled? Not at all! Christ points us to himself. He doesn't ask us to focus the eyes of our faith on some thousand-year-long earthly kingdom ruled over by him. When he comes again, he will not make us citizens of a kingdom in which the traces and effects of sin have not as yet been completely wiped out. The words of Paul in Philippians 3:20,21 assure us of that: "Our citizenship is in heaven. And we eagerly await a Savior from there, the Lord Jesus

Christ, who, by the power that enables him to bring everything under his control, will transform our lowly bodies so that they will be like his glorious body."

Christ's kingdom is a present kingdom

Yet it would seem, wouldn't it, as though the millennialists and we at least agree that Christ's kingdom is still a matter of the future. Nothing could be further from the truth. We believe that Scripture teaches that our Lord Jesus Christ rules as King today as well as in eternity.

Millennialists are not comfortable with that teaching of Scripture because they have altered what Scripture says about the kingdom of Christ in order to make room for their millennium. According to them, our Lord Jesus Christ at his first coming actually failed to accomplish what he had come to do. At that time, according to some millennialists, he came to establish a temporal world power, offer it to the Jews, and then, when they rejected it, postponed it to a thousand-year period after his second advent. As evidence they like to point to John 1:11: "He came to that which was his own, but his own did not receive him." In his book *Jesus Is Coming,* William E. Blackstone, a millennialist of the early years of this century, states, "He would have set up the Kingdom but they rejected and crucified Him" (page 87).

It is true that the leaders of Israel rejected Christ and crucified him, but it is not true that he offered them an earthly kingdom. In fact, it was the other way around. The people wanted to force an earthly kingdom upon him, and it was he who resisted. We read in John 6:14,15, "After the people saw the miraculous sign that Jesus did, they began to say, 'Surely this is the Prophet who is to come into the world.' Jesus, knowing that they intended to come and make him king by force, withdrew again to a mountain by himself." That's quite a different story, isn't it!

But that doesn't mean that Christ did not offer them a kingdom. In Mark 1:14,15 we read, "After John was put in prison, Jesus went into Galilee, proclaiming the good news of God. 'The time has come,' he said. 'The kingdom of God is near. Repent and believe the good news!'" These words of the evangelist and of the Lord show us both what kind of a kingdom it is of which Christ is the King and how this kingdom is built. The kingdom of God, the reigning and ruling activity of our Lord here on earth, takes place when the gospel is proclaimed and people believe. That kingdom is in existence now. Christ tells us that the time for its inauguration was fulfilled. It was not delayed to a time one thousand years before the end of the world.

To teach that it was delayed violates not only the above text but also many others. Among them is Colossians 1:12-14: "Giving thanks to the Father, who has qualified you to share in the inheritance of the saints in the kingdom of light [a fine description of heaven!]. For he has rescued us from the dominion of darkness and brought us into the kingdom of the Son he loves [now, not at some future date], in whom we have redemption, the forgiveness of sins [that's the blessed nature of Christ's kingdom!]." We are in that kingdom now through faith in Jesus Christ. There is another phase, that's clear, but that phase does not take place on earth but in heaven. There simply is no room for a millennial kingdom in these plain words of Holy Scripture.

Not an earthly kingdom

The previous passages also help us understand Jesus' answers to Pilate. The accusation brought against Jesus was that he had made himself a king, suggesting that he was a rival of Caesar. Christ admitted that he was a King but not that kind of king—not an earthly king. He said to Pilate, "My kingdom is not of this world. If it were, my servants would fight to prevent my arrest by the Jews. But now my kingdom is from another place" (John 18:36). Christ did not say that his kingdom lay in the future. It was present on earth then, and he even had servants. But the nature of the kingdom was spiritual.

We cannot blame Pilate, the politician, for not being able to understand Christ. Pilate's next question was a natural: Are you a king then? It is unbelievable that students of Scripture should be unable to understand the Lord's next words and, in spite of them, urge us to be on the alert for the beginning of a millennial kingdom with Christ as a great earthly king. Christ, in his words to Pilate, even decides the time element for us: "You are right in saying I am a king. In fact, for this reason I was born, and for this I came into the world, to testify to the truth. Everyone on the side of truth listens to me" (John 18:37). Jesus' kingdom began with his incarnation, and it was not a political kingdom.

But the millennialists aren't any more satisfied with Jesus' answer than Pilate was. They insist on an earthly kingdom one thousand years before the end of time. In his book *World Aflame,* Billy Graham says, "A new world is being born. A new social order will emerge when Christ comes back to set up His Kingdom. Swords will be turned into pruning hooks, and the lion will lie down with the lamb. A fabulous future is on the way" (page 185). In fact, he calls it a utopia (page 180).

Don't be taken in!

But is the alleged millennial kingdom really that good? Dr. Graham insists, "The longing and dreams of mankind will be fulfilled, as God establishes His glorious Kingdom on earth for the enjoyment of mankind" (page 182). Hal Lindsey, in *The Late Great Planet Earth,* states, "All men will have plenty and be secure. There will be a chicken in every pot and no one will steal it! The Great Society, which human rulers throughout the centuries have promised but never produced, will at last be realized under Christ's rule" (page 177).

Not bad, until you begin to analyze the total picture these men paint of the millennium. Then it begins to lose part of its appeal—even for the flesh. Graham says: "The second coming of Christ will be so revolutionary that it will change every aspect of life on this planet. Christ will reign in righteousness. Disease will be arrested. Death will be modified. War will be abolished. Nature will be changed. Man will live as it was originally intended he should live" (page 178). Sounds good? Note that you will still be a sinner, still get sick, and still die. Note the words in the quotation: *arrested, modified.* Later Graham speaks of this alleged millennium as a time "when disease and death would be almost nonexistent!" (page 193) and "when sin and its evil deeds would be limited and restricted" (page 194). Sigh! Lindsey agrees, "Christ establishes the millennial kingdom and the surviving believers go into it as mortals and repopulate the earth" (page 178). And it ends with a rebellion, a war: "At the end of a thousand years the unbelieving children rebel; Christ judges them" (page 178). So basically it's the same merry-go-round again. Even sin! Another sigh!

If this is all Christ will bring us for a thousand years before he takes us to the sinless existence with him, then there is no real sense in what Paul wrote in Colossians: "Set your minds on things above, not on earthly things" (3:2) and "When Christ, who is your life, appears, then you also will appear with him in glory" (3:4). Millennialists neither follow the admonition of verse 2 nor offer us the promise of verse 4.

So far, of course, we have not taken a close look at Revelation 20, the passage millennialists look upon as the cornerstone of their strange doctrine. Whatever the millennium of Revelation may be, it is only after the millennium has come to an end that the words of the Spirit of God to John in Revelation 21:3,4 will go into effect: "I heard a loud voice from the throne saying, 'Now the dwelling of God is with men, and he will live with them. They will be his people, and God himself will be with them and be their God. He will wipe every tear from their eyes. There will be no more death or mourning or crying or pain, for the old order of things has passed away.'" Surely, the alleged millennium suffers by comparison.

Before we take a closer look at Revelation 20, we must consider the Old Testament prophecies with which millennialists so liberally pack their writings. They are especially apt to point to the return of the Jews to Israel and say, "See! You're wrong about the millennium. It's all coming to pass just as we said."

Before you let yourself be taken in by their misinterpretations of Scripture, remind yourself of the fact that Christ insists that he is a King now, that we who believe in him are members of his kingdom now, and that when he comes again it will be to receive us into glory, not to establish an earthly kingdom that admittedly isn't perfect even though he is perfect. Christ has something better for us than that!

III

The Millennium—Was It Prophesied?

Undoubtedly you would like to see things better than they are. Undoubtedly you would like to live a lot longer and have more of the good things of this world to enjoy. Undoubtedly you would like to be in a position of power and authority. Undoubtedly you would like to see righteousness prevail on this earth, instead of witnessing a rise in the number of criminal acts and in lawlessness. Is this a possibility?

Many well-known religious teachers offer the millennium as the Lord's answer to what your heart so greatly desires. But in chapter 2 of this booklet, we examined the millennium and, to our surprise, discovered that it left a lot to be desired. The coming millennium would not rid the earth and mankind completely of sin, death, or even war. In other words, the millennium falls woefully short of being the real answer to human yearnings.

Could it be that we might have erred in our analysis? It's clear that a basic question remains to be answered: Is the millennium something that God has promised, that he has prophesied in his Word?

The millennium and Israel

There is particularly one issue on the basis of which the millennium will be found either wanting or valid. That's Israel.

As you have perhaps noticed in reading books such as *The Late Great Planet Earth,* most millennialists teach that the people of Israel are to have a special place in the future millennial kingdom of Christ. In fact, millennialists take most of the promises given the descendants of Abraham in Scripture and apply them as referring to the Jews at the time of the millennium or shortly before. So the question we must settle on the basis of Scripture is this: Does God have a special plan for the Jewish people at the end of time?

Millennialists point to present events in world politics as a direct fulfillment of prophecy. Among them is the establishing of the modern state of Israel in 1948 and then the Six Days' War in 1967, when Israel added immensely to its territory. According to millennialists, these events are all evidence of the nearness of Christ's second coming and of the millennium.

Hal Lindsey states in *The Late Great Planet Earth,* "The central theme of the Jewish prophets was that 'the Messiah' would come and fulfill the promises given to their forefathers, Abraham, Isaac, and Jacob. In these promises Israel is to be the leading nation in the world under the reign of the Messiah who would bring universal peace, prosperity, and harmony among all people of the earth" (page 28).

That Christ did not accomplish this at his first coming is clear from history. Mr. Lindsey insists that he will do so at his second coming. But the real question remains: Did God ever really promise this?

Mr. Lindsey is convinced that God did. He points excitedly to the creation of the nation of Israel: "Israel a nation—a dream for so many years, made a reality on 14 May 1948 when David Ben-Gurion read the Declaration of Independence announcing the establishment of a Jewish nation to be known as the State of Israel" (page 43). An additional factor in his line of argument is Israel's 1967 repossession of old Jerusalem: "Then came the war of June, 1967—the phenomenal Israel six-day blitz. I was personally puzzled as to the significance of it all until the third day of fighting when Moshe Dayan, the ingenious Israeli general, marched to the wailing wall, the last remnant of the Old Temple, and said, 'We have returned to our holiest of holy places, never to leave her again'" (page 55). For Lindsey, the next step on God's timetable is the rebuilding of the temple.

All this sounds very plausible, even the Scripture passages he quotes. But one needs to ask whether this is what the prophets, and later the Lord and his apostles, were actually speaking about. Let's check.

A great silence

At this point of the discussion, it's a good idea to scan Revelation 20. This chapter, as you know, is the basic passage for all millennialists. It is the only portion of Scripture that speaks of the "thousand years," that period which the millennialists have appropriated for their own special doctrine.

Search as we will, there is no hint in Revelation 20 about a restoration of Israel to the Holy Land or the presence of the temple. Regardless of how this chapter may be interpreted, these factors, so important to the doctrine of the millennialists, are simply missing. Such a lapse is indefensible considering that millennialists make the existence of Israel as a nation a prerequisite for the millennial reign of Christ on earth.

Romans 9 and 11

But doesn't Paul speak about the restoration of Israel? At first glance it seems so. Most millennialists insist that with the arrival of the millennium, all living Jews will be converted to Jesus Christ. In support of their teaching, they like to point to Romans 11:25,26: "I do not want you to be ignorant of this mystery, brothers, so that you may not be conceited: Israel has experienced a hardening in part until the full number of the Gentiles has come in. And so all Israel will be saved."

What about the words "all Israel"? Don't they sound as though at least all Israelites living at that time will be converted to Christ? Before we accept this explanation, it will be well to ask what Paul understands by the words "all Israel." He defines the term in Romans 9. He takes up the objection that God seemingly has not fulfilled his promises to Israel of old and that, therefore, further fulfillment is needed if God is to be a God of truth. Paul does indeed speak of the Israelites: "Theirs is the adoption as sons; theirs the divine glory, the covenants, the receiving of the law, the temple worship and the promises" (9:4). It was, of course, evident in Paul's day that God had not showered upon Israel the blessings they had expected according to their reading of the Old Testament. Their lot—under the Romans—left a lot to be desired. Consequently, they were looking for a worldly Messiah.

Those who teach a millennium use the same argument: God has not as yet fully carried out his promises. All of Israel, according to them, needs to be brought into the kingdom of God. What these teachers fail to do is to consider Paul's own answer. He writes in Romans 9:6-8: "It is not as though God's word had failed. For not all who are descended from Israel are Israel. Nor because they are his descendants are they all Abraham's children. On the contrary, 'It is through Isaac that your offspring will be reckoned.' In other words, it is not the natural children who are God's children, but it is the children of the promise who are regarded as Abraham's offspring." So "all Israel" means all those among the descendants of Abraham who come to faith in Jesus Christ together with all Gentiles who come to the same faith. Of a general conversion of the Jews before the end of the world or at the coming of the millennium, Paul knows nothing at all. He only knows of the conversion of a remnant, who over the centuries turn to the Lord.

In Paul's words "And so all Israel will be saved" (Romans 11:26), there is another important word, one that clearly demonstrates that the millennialist point of view simply cannot hold. Millennialists understand this passage in this way: During the New Testament time, the gospel is preached to the Gentiles; then after all of the elect among the Gentiles are converted and brought to faith, the conversion of all of Israel will take place. Notice that they are really translating the text to read: "And then all Israel will be saved." Only it doesn't say that in English, and it doesn't say that in the original Greek. It says, "And *so* all Israel will be saved," meaning, "in that way." The Israel Paul is speaking about here is the full number of the elect—both Gentile and Jew. Although the greater part of Israel as such always rejects the Lord Jesus, during all the years the gospel is being preached to the Gentiles (the New Testament period), a remnant in Israel will also believe. The result is that all the elect ("all Israel") will come to faith by the time judgment day arrives for this world of ours and the Lord Jesus appears in the clouds of heaven.

Old Testament prophecies

With the previous as background, it will not be necessary to discuss all of the Old Testament prophecies individually or in detail. A teaching that is not accepted in the New Testament cannot be found in the Old Testament either. Yet a few words of explanation are in order.

Millennialists appeal particularly to the prophecies of Isaiah, Jeremiah, Ezekiel, and Daniel. A careful reading of these prophets will show that much of what they say applies to the New Testament church. However, when it is the actual physical and national restoration of Israel that is meant, we must never forget that these prophets wrote before, during, and shortly before the final end of the exile. Israel's return from exile is never divided by the prophets into two phases, separated by the time of the New Testament. It takes place before the Messiah's first coming.

The Old Testament itself closes with a message from the prophet Malachi. It is noteworthy that this prophet does not speak about a return of the Jews but only of the coming of the Messiah and of repentance on the part of the people. Why doesn't he speak of a return of the people of Israel to the Holy Land? Because he wrote it after the close of the exile. This is a clear indication that the words of the previous prophets concerning a return of Israel envisioned the return from the exile, not a millennium.

Conditioned promises

Millennialists, of course, reject this explanation. They say that God promised so much more than what was fulfilled in the return from the exile. God did. But we ought to note that God's promises were conditional. There was always an *if.*

God reveals in Jeremiah 18:7-10 the rule and principle he follows: "If at any time I announce that a nation or kingdom is to be uprooted, torn down and destroyed, and if that nation I warned repents of its evil, then I will relent and not inflict on it the disaster I had planned. And if at another time I announce that a nation or kingdom is to be built up and planted, and if it does evil in my sight and does not obey me, then I will reconsider the good I had intended to do for it." That this principle also applied to God's dealing with Israel is clear from the very next words, for there God himself applies it to Israel.

The promises given to Israel before and during the exile were marvelous, but they were always conditional. You will not notice that unless you read more than the individual verses that the millennialists quote so tellingly. Israel did not abide by the conditions that God set down in his dealing with them. We need only turn again to that last book of the

Old Testament, the book of Malachi, to see how utterly Israel failed to do so. And when Christ came the first time, John tells us, "He came to that which was his own, but his own did not receive him" (John 1:11).

Other considerations

In this very connection, we should not forget that the Old Testament prophets also spoke of the New Covenant and of the church and that many of the promises to which millennialists point as supporting their theory are represented in the New Testament as being fulfilled in Christ's New Testament people. Before any of us accept the interpretations given by those who preach a millennium, we ought to read the passages they quote very carefully in their broader context to see whom God was really addressing.

Above all, we must keep in mind what is revealed in the New Testament. The Old Testament is not an isolated piece of writing. Nor for that matter, the New Testament. After his resurrection, our Lord said to his disciples: "This is what I told you while I was still with you: Everything must be fulfilled that is written about me in the Law of Moses, the Prophets and the Psalms" (Luke 24:44). To make the Old Testament Scriptures into something Christ does not say would be to misinterpret them.

Sooner or later those who teach a millennium fall into the very danger against which Jesus himself warned, the danger of date setting. Hal Lindsey does so when he states: "Jesus Christ predicted an event which would trigger a time of unparalleled catastrophe for the Jewish nation shortly before his second coming. This 'abomination of desolation' or desecration of the inner sanctum of the Temple would occur at the midway point of God's last seven years of dealing with the Jewish people before setting up the long-awaited Kingdom of God" (page 56). According to this, someday soon we will know almost to a day when our Lord will appear at his second coming. But Christ says, "No one knows about that day or hour" (Matthew 24:36).

Millennialists also insist that the Word of God requires that before Christ can return a second time, the temple at Jerusalem must be rebuilt and the Old Testament sacrifices reinstituted. According to that, we are rather safe in thinking that Christ won't be coming for a while yet, aren't we! How does this agree with the words of Christ, who said, "So you also must be ready, because the Son of Man will come at an hour when you do not expect him" (Matthew 24:44)? How many do you suppose will be unprepared for his coming because of the teaching of the millennialists?

But what if Israel were to rebuild the temple and reinstitute the old worship forms? In doing so, they would neither fulfill any Old Testament prophecies nor institute a way of worship acceptable to God. To teach otherwise is to set aside the sacrifice offered by our Lord Jesus Christ. It would be the very opposite of what God is teaching us in Hebrews 9 and 10. Don't permit yourself to be misled. The millennium is simply not taught in either of the Testaments. Neither the Old Testament nor the New Testament has any prophecies that foretell it.

IV

Will the True Millennium Please Stand Up?

When we listen to the stories told by millennialists about what the millennium will supposedly be like, we see that their stories in no way resemble what Scripture teaches in Revelation 20 and elsewhere. In fact, no two millennialists come up with exactly the same tale. Charles E. Brown put it well in *The Hope of His Coming:* "What with the great tribulation, the parousia, the rapture, the aeons, the remnant, eight covenants, seven dispensations, three comings of Christ, four judgment days, two endings of the world, several sets of last days, and three resurrections, I submit there has been grafted into the simple Word of God an elaborate system of interpretation which could never occur to the ordinary believer through an unbiased reading of his Bible" (page 71). We do well to listen to what Scripture and, in particular, Revelation 20 actually say.

The book of Revelation

In the year A.D. 70, Jerusalem was destroyed by the Romans, and the Jews were slaughtered and scattered. God was no longer dealing directly and almost exclusively with one nation only, but as demonstrated by the book of Acts, the gospel message was being proclaimed to all people, Jew and Gentile alike.

Some 20 years later, the Lord Jesus Christ appeared to his servant John, who was in exile on the island of Patmos. Christ had a message to transmit to his servants, the believers, through John. Since these were words of prophecy, they were written in such a way that their meaning could only be unlocked by the proper use of the rest of Scripture, particularly the words of Jesus himself. In this way the book of Revelation is very much like the books of the Old Testament prophets.

Figurative language

Naturally, this involved the use of a great deal of figurative, picturesque language. Consider, for example, the description of Jesus in Revelation 1:12-16: "I turned around to see the voice that was speaking to me. And when I turned I saw seven golden lampstands, and among the lampstands was someone 'like a son of man,' dressed in a robe reaching down to his feet and with a golden sash around his chest. His head and hair were white like wool, as white as snow, and his eyes were like blazing fire. His feet were like bronze glowing in a furnace, and his voice was like the sound of rushing waters. In his right hand he held seven stars, and out of his mouth came a sharp double-edged sword. His face was like the sun shining in all its brilliance."

Is this how Jesus will appear on the Last Day? Hardly! He will indeed appear in glory, and yet the angels at the ascension said, "This same Jesus, who has been taken from you into heaven, will come back in the same way you have seen him go into heaven" (Acts 1:11). What John saw in Revelation was a vision, not a photograph. A vision is always an interpretation. It seeks to deepen our understanding. This is true throughout the book of Revelation, with its many visions of beasts and living beings and its nonmathematical use of numbers. We must constantly be aware of this as we read the book of Revelation.

Unfortunately, many interpreters have ignored this fact and have thus come up with interpretations of Revelation 20 that do violence to the rest of Scripture, particularly to our Lord's own description of the end of the world. It is not reasonable that in Revelation our Lord would contradict what he had prophesied while he was among us, for that would make him a liar. His own words, therefore, must be used to test the interpretations of those who would explain any part of the book of Revelation.

"And I saw"

One of the recurring phrases in the book of Revelation that separates one vision from another is the phrase "And I saw" (sometimes simply "I saw" in the NIV) and, at times, "And I heard." These words should always alert the reader that something new is about to be shown or explained.

The words "And I saw" occur four times in chapter 20. The first covers verses 1-3: "And I saw" Satan bound for a thousand years. The second takes place in verses 4-10:

"I saw" the saints reigning with Christ a thousand years, after which time Satan is loosed for a little while and finally cast into the lake of fire to be tormented forever. Then in verse 11, "I saw" introduces the great white throne with Christ, the judge. In the next verse, "And I saw" introduces the vision of those who stand before the throne to be judged, "the dead, great and small."

The thousand years

All portions of chapter 20 stand in a definite relationship to a period of time called a thousand years. The first portion tells what happens to Satan at the beginning of the one-thousand-year period and at its close. The second portion relates what happens to the saints during the one thousand years and at its close. The third portion reveals what happens at the end of the one thousand years. For us, the real question, then, is whether this thousand-year period is the millennium of the millennialists or not?

According to the millennialists, this thousand-year period is exactly one thousand years of 365 days each. Is this interpretation valid?

It is clear that in Revelation 20 Christ relates this thousand-year period to the end of the world. But in Matthew 25:13 he said, "Keep watch, because you do not know the day or the hour" when Christ will return. If the thousand years of Revelation 20 were an exact figure, they would make mockery of Jesus' words in Matthew 25, for at least the people at the end of the first century would have known that the Lord wasn't coming back for at least a thousand years. Christ would thus be contradicting himself.

But in Revelation 20, this number is clearly used in a figurative sense. Those who insist that it is exactly one thousand earth years should look at the context in which the expression is used. If the thousand years are to be understood literally, then surely all other items must also be understood literally. Do they so understand them? Do they insist that Satan is bound with actual chains made of metal? Hardly! Again, where is there a bottomless pit on earth, and is that seal an actual seal like the seal Pilate approved for the tomb of Jesus?

It is clear that all this is figurative when we note that Revelation 20:3 indicates that Satan is restricted, or bound, in one area of his operation only, namely, "to keep him from deceiving the nations anymore until the thousand years were ended." During the Old Testament, God dealt principally with one nation only, the nation of Israel. All other nations followed the deceptive voice of Satan. He was prince of this world. When did this change? It changed when Christ died on the cross and then arose from the dead to send his disciples out to all nations to preach the gospel. Though the devil prowls around "like a roaring lion looking for someone to devour" (I Peter 5:8), yet Satan was from that moment on severely hampered in trying to block the preaching of the gospel. Thus our Lord in this portion of Revelation 20 indicates when this thousand-year period began. It's clearly not after his second coming. It began with his first coming.

Christ's reign

What about the second vision in Revelation 20 (verses 4-6)? Doesn't that indicate that the thousand years is a period when Christ reigns here on earth with his resurrected saints? So say the millennialists. But Revelation 20 does not support that teaching.

The second vision is the vision of the saints (martyrs and confessors) reigning with Christ a thousand years. Where? On earth? No! The word used is *souls*—souls that lived and reigned with Christ. Souls are not resurrected persons. During these thousand years, the bodies remained where they were put to rest, but the souls reigned with Christ. It is clear that this is a picture of souls in heaven with the Lord Jesus. Note that the words used are "they lived" not "they lived again." ("Lived" more accurately reflects the original Greek than the NIV's "came to life.") And it is this living and reigning with Christ that is then called the "first resurrection." Over these souls the second death (hell) will have no power. Though on the final day these souls will be reunited with their bodies and stand in the judgment, they cannot come into condemnation. They will then be acknowledged publicly before the whole world as people whose names are written in the book of life.

This is not the millennium of the millennialists. This is a vision of the glory and joy of those who, one by one, have been rescued out of the hands of Satan and whose souls through the first death have been transferred to glory to live and reign with Christ. How long is this millennium? For all practical purposes, it is coextensive with the New Testament period.

We are thus living in the millennium now. Satan's hands have been tied so that we, though members of a nation on the other side of the globe, have heard and believed the gospel and have the assurance that our souls will be with

Christ after death and that the final judgment cannot harm us. In fact, should we be living at the time when it comes, Jesus tells us, "When these things begin to take place, stand up and lift up your heads, because your redemption is drawing near" (Luke 21:28).

A little season

What's ahead? As the thousand-year period of Revelation 20 ends, Satan is loosed for a while. Again he seeks to persuade the nations to resist the gospel, to make war on the saints. Could it be possible that that period of time has already begun? It would almost seem so, for paganism is raising its head as never before. Atheism has become a real power. The black arts are even gaining the minds of the intellectuals. Many nations have taken a hard stand against Christian missionaries. And within the outward church itself, one denomination after another is rejecting basic Christian doctrines. Professing Christians too are making common cause with the world. But—there are still doors opening where the gospel is being preached. We are quite aware of how God in his grace is making use of our synod in proclaiming the gospel during these days, whose character we are wondering about. Perhaps it was days like these that the Savior was talking about when he said, "Then you will be handed over to be persecuted and put to death, and you will be hated by all nations because of me. At that time many will turn away from the faith and will betray and hate each other, and many false prophets will appear and deceive many people. Because of the increase of wickedness, the love of most will grow cold" (Matthew 24:9-12). But note also the promise that follows: "But he who stands firm to the end will be saved" (Matthew 24:13).

However, it is Christ alone who determines when the words he spoke in that very connection are fulfilled, saying, "This gospel of the kingdom will be preached in the whole world as a testimony to all nations, and then the end will come" (Matthew 24:14). Then the millennium of Revelation 20 will have come to a glorious close—Satan and his cohorts consigned to hell, Christ and the saints in the new heaven and new earth of Revelation 21 and 22.

Will the true millennium please stand up? Read Revelation 20 as is, without importing ideas that are not in the text but permitting your understanding to be guided by what Jesus said while on earth, and you too will agree that the millennium is now. More than that, this fact is a real source of joy in our work for Christ here on earth and the comfort we need when we face the first death. Don't let those who with a show of wisdom preach another kind of millennium rob you of what Christ wants to assure you of in Revelation 20!

V

What About the Rapture?

Perhaps you have heard about the two-thousand-member congregation in North Hollywood, California, that includes in its bylaws constitutional provisions for continued leadership of the church if its officers were suddenly taken to heaven. An article of the bylaws of First Assembly of God Church reads: "The blessed hope . . . clearly speaks of an instantaneous and general translation of members of the assembly. All pastors, deacons, elders, and other . . . leaders and officers are expected to be caught up alive in a moment of time, thus depriving the church of duly constituted legal representation. In such an event the remaining members . . . shall meet in an emergency church council the following Sunday at 11 A.M. and elect . . . a temporary chairman." Members have also been urged to rewrite their wills and insurance policies naming the church as beneficiary. Since Assembly of God churches generally teach that those raptured will go to heaven for seven years and then return at the millennium to rule on earth with Christ for one thousand years, one can say that the North Hollywood congregation is at least living up to its creed. More important, however, is the need to determine whether its creed agrees with Scripture.

Sensational

Descriptions of the so-called rapture are startling, to say the least. One of the more sober discussions is that by Tim LaHaye, Baptist pastor and coauthor of the popular Left Behind series of books. He writes in *The Beginning of the End,* "The Rapture of the Church will be an event of such startling proportions that the entire world will be conscious of our leaving. Some have suggested that there will be airplane, bus, and train wrecks throughout the world when Christian operators are suddenly taken out of the world. Who can imagine the chaos of the freeways when automobile drivers are snatched out of their cars!" It's easy to let your imagination run wild. But again, is this really the way it will be?

Who teaches this?

Many agree with Tim LaHaye. You will recognize the names of Billy Graham and Hal Lindsey, to whom we have referred before in this booklet. Even quite a few members of the Creation Research Society, well-known to us, promote all these teachings, though they are contrary to Scripture. These doctrines are current in most evangelical and conservative Protestant circles.

The Lutheran Confessions reject these teachings, but that has not prevented some Lutherans from advocating them. Pastors of conservative Lutheran churches relate that occasionally some of their members have been misled by what they hear over radio and TV and read in popular books. Our members are not immune. That's why it's necessary for us to go back to Scripture again and again.

First Thessalonians

Those who teach a rapture appeal to First Thessalonians 4:13-18:

> Brothers, we do not want you to be ignorant about those who fall asleep, or to grieve like the rest of men, who have no hope. We believe that Jesus died and rose again and so we believe that God will bring with Jesus those who have fallen asleep in him. According to the Lord's own word, we tell you that we who are still alive, who are left till the coming of the Lord, will certainly not precede those who have fallen asleep. For the Lord himself will come down from heaven, with a loud command, with the voice of the archangel and with the trumpet call of God, and the dead in Christ will rise first. After that, we who are still alive and are left will be caught up together with them in the clouds to meet the Lord in the air. And so we will be with the Lord forever. Therefore encourage each other with these words.

Is this the seven-year rapture?

But does this passage say that the Christian dead who are raised and the Christians who are living at that time will be removed from this world for a period of seven years and then return to earth at the beginning of the millennium?

There is no hint of anything like that in this passage or in the rest of the epistle. In First Thessalonians, Paul writes very frequently about the second coming of Christ. Not once, however, does Paul indicate that this coming is in two stages and that in the first stage, Christ will come only partway to earth. First Thessalonains 4:17 does not speak of a *remaining* in the air but of a *meeting* there.

First Thessalonians speaks of the coming of our Lord Jesus Christ as the coming of "his Son from heaven" (1:10) and as a coming of "our Lord Jesus . . . with all his holy ones" (3:13). The day of the Lord is also described as coming like a thief in the night (5:2). Second Thessalonians, written shortly after First Thessalonians, speaks of that day as the moment when the Lord Jesus will be revealed from heaven with his mighty angels, in blazing fire punishing those who do not know God and do not obey the gospel (1:7,8). It teaches that these people will be punished with everlasting destruction when Christ comes to be glorified in his holy people and to be marveled at among those who have believed (1:9,10). There is not the slightest hint that these are two events separated by a number of years. It is the great judgment day, which for us Christians is the day when we enter heaven body and soul.

Those who speak of a seven-year rapture when Christ and Christians are in the air above the earth (or, according to others, in heaven) while there is tribulation on earth, during which others are still brought to the Christian faith, are forced to read this into the text. The plain words of Scripture do not support their teaching.

How secret?

There are also some other considerations that show this to be an impossible doctrine. Read the words of First Thessalonians again: "The Lord himself will come down from heaven, with a loud command, with the voice of the archangel and with the trumpet call of God" (4:16). Someone has called this verse the noisiest in Scripture. True, but those who teach the so-called rapture must silence this shout and voice and trumpet call so that all do not hear it. They do so very artfully, but without a single shred of evidence from Scripture.

Here is how Bill McKee in *Orbit of Ashes* does it: "The shout of Jesus—a shout of joy—summons earth's Christians to their tryst in the sky. We are his bride, his blood-bought possession, and he's coming to take us home. The archangel peals a cry of victory *in the language of the soul,* confirming our faith and hope in our heavenly destiny. And the trumpet of God splits the sky—though only *those on the right frequency will hear the call.*"

Just where in Scripture do you read anything like that? In fact, here is what Jesus said: "Do not be amazed at this, for a time is coming when *all who are in their graves will hear his voice* and come out—those who have done good will rise to live, and those who have done evil will rise to be condemned" (John 5:28,29). Notice that the wicked dead and the believing dead both hear that voice. There is no indication of an interval between their rising.

Why only the believers?

To support their false exegesis, those who believe in a seven-year rapture, followed by a millennium, before the wicked are raised ask why First Thessalonians says nothing about the wicked dead. That's clear from the passage itself. The Thessalonians had either misunderstood Paul or forgotten what he had taught them. Consequently, when some of their fellow believers died before the Lord's return, they feared that these loved ones of theirs would not share the glory of that great day. Paul assured them that the Christians living at that time would "certainly not precede those who have fallen asleep" (4:15). Because he was writing to comfort believers, he said very little directly about the ungodly dead. However, he did not ignore them. In the next chapter, he spoke of that day again: "While people are saying, 'Peace and safety,' destruction will come on them suddenly, as labor pains on a pregnant woman, and they will not escape" (5:3). God, however, has not appointed us to suffer his wrath (5:9). Paul wanted to assure the Thessalonians that "whether we are awake or asleep, we may live together with him" (5:10). That's why he put the emphasis where he did.

Yes, we expect to be separated from the wicked, but on the same day when the wicked will be consigned to hell. On that day the Lord will demonstrate his goodness to his believers and will bring eternal punishment upon the unbelievers. "They will go away to eternal punishment, but the righteous to eternal life" (Matthew 25:46) are his own words. In fact, our Lord himself has clearly indicated on what day he will raise us. He states in John 6:40: "My Father's will is that everyone who looks to the Son and believes in him shall have eternal life, and I will raise him up at the last day." It's on that day that we go to meet him. Nor will that be something temporary. "So we will be with the Lord forever," writes Paul in First Thessalonians 4:17.

VI

What About the "Great Tribulation"?

It's a troubled world in which we live, and Scripture makes no promise that it will improve. As Christians we have the commission to proclaim the gospel of Jesus Christ, but since the preaching of the gospel confronts man with his sins, the unbelieving world has often caused the Christian to bear the brunt of its hatred against Christ. Christ himself predicted this when he said, "If the world hates you, keep in mind that it hated me first. If you belonged to the world, it would love you as its own. As it is, you do not belong to the world, but I have chosen you out of the world. That is why the world hates you. Remember the words I spoke to you: 'No servant is greater than his master.' If they persecuted me, they will persecute you also" (John 15:18-20).

The apostle Paul and his coworkers reminded the people of Lystra, Iconium, and Antioch of that same truth when they exhorted them to remain true to the faith, saying, "We must go through many hardships [KJV: "much tribulation"] to enter the kingdom of God" (Acts 14:22). Since hardships (tribulation) are something to be expected, it does not surprise us that the book of Revelation describes the saved who have died and who are with Christ as those who have "come out of the great tribulation; they have washed their robes and made them white in the blood of the Lamb" (Revelation 7:14). Nor does the description that Christ gives of the end of the world promise anything better. It is remarkable that our Lord in his teaching never—never—says anything about a golden period, let's say of a thousand years duration, in which we Christians before the end of the world will rule in earthly splendor with him on this globe of ours. To interpret the words of Revelation 20 in that way contradicts everything Christ has said elsewhere.

The fact that Christ speaks of the whole life of the Christian as being subject to tribulation, with no sign of a letup, puts those who teach a millennium on the spot. That's why they have invented the teaching of the rapture as their way of exempting Christians from the horrors of what they teach as the "Great Tribulation." It soon becomes evident that they have torn these Scripture passages entirely out of their context. One of the passages of which they claim teaches a special tribulation period at the end of the world from which Christians will be exempt is Matthew 24:21: "Then there will be great distress [KJV: "tribulation"], unequaled from the beginning of the world until now—and never to be equaled again." Regardless of what the true explanation of this passage is—and we'll come back to it later—the next verse clearly states that believers (the elect) are present in the tribulation, for Christ says, "If those days had not been cut short, no one would survive, but for the sake of the elect those days will be shortened" (verse 22). To teach as they do concerning the rapture and the "Great Tribulation," millennialists simply have to ignore this verse. Thus it becomes evident that their teaching is not scriptural, even though they insist that it is. Let's not be taken in by it.

The "Great Tribulation"

What do millennialists actually claim when they teach the "Great Tribulation"? There are so many variations on this theme that it is almost impossible to give a fair account of what is taught. Basically, they teach that after the true believers are taken by Christ in a rapture either to heaven or somewhere out in space, there will follow a time of unequaled tribulation through which Jews and Gentiles and the professing church (those left behind at the rapture) will pass. They teach that this period of time will be exactly seven years in duration and that it will be divided into two equal periods of three and one-half years each. During the first three and one-half years, the Antichrist will make a covenant with the Jews whereby temple worship will be restored. Also during this time, a group of Jewish evangelists will put on the most successful evangelism program the world has ever seen, despite the fact that in the rapture the Holy Spirit too has been taken away from the earth. In a period of slightly more than 1,200 days, these evangelists will be more successful than the Christian church and the Holy Spirit were in a space of 2,000 years. At the end of that period, however, the covenant will be broken and a time of unparalleled persecution and destruction will break upon the world, until suddenly Christ comes to establish the millennium.

Nowhere do we find anything like this even hinted at in Christ's words. The passages that are quoted to support the various elements in the previous composite picture are manifestly misused. Before we turn to Christ's own description of the end, particularly as given in Matthew 24, we want to call attention to two specific items. First, the teaching about a successful evangelism program without the presence and activity of the Holy Spirit is something completely unbiblical. Scripture teaches us in I Corinthians 12:3 that "no one can say, 'Jesus is Lord,' except by the Holy Spirit." Suggesting the contrary should alert us that there is something seriously wrong with the millennialists' doctrine of the "Great Tribulation." Second, this doctrine of theirs actually provides the unbeliever with a second chance, and thus is somewhat related to the Roman Catholic idea of a purgatory. That too is unbiblical.

Christ's Olivet discourse

By far the most detailed passage in which Christ speaks about the end of the world is his discourse to his disciples on the Mount of Olives, recorded in Matthew 24 and 25, Mark 13, and Luke 21. Christ and his disciples had just left Jerusalem, where he had said of that city and nation, "Look, your house is left to you desolate" (Matthew 23:38). When the disciples called his attention to some of the grand structures, almost wondering out loud how these could be left desolate, Jesus told them that "not one stone here will be left on another; every one will be thrown down" (Matthew 24:2). It was then that they asked him, "Tell us . . . when will this happen, and what will be the sign of your coming and of the end of the age?" (verse 3).

Jesus answered by beginning with the last part of the question and pointed out that in the years ahead (the years of the New Testament period) as the world approaches its end, there will be plenty of signs—abnormal things happening in human society, in nature, and in the church—that should alert the believer to be ready for Christ's coming. Over the years these signs have been fulfilled any number of times, including the very last of them: "This gospel of the kingdom will be preached in the whole world as a testimony to all nations, and then the end will come" (verse 14). The entire account, however, shows that the lot of Christians throughout this period of time will be anything but an easy one. Not only does the history of the Christian church demonstrate that, but it isn't any different now. We indeed live in a country where persecution is of the subtle rather than the crass kind, but not all believers are that fortunate in this world of ours. The signs spoken of by Christ are all around us. We should be alert for the Lord at all times.

In all of these words from the lips of our Lord there is no mention of a special seven-year period just before the millennium when a special measure of tribulation will be poured out upon the world, a tribulation, however, that we Christians will escape. There is no hint of anything like that. What special troubles may mark the "short time" (Revelation 20:3) when Satan is loosed at the very end, we commit into the Lord's hands. It is certainly possible that conditions may become much worse for the church of God before the end; yet if Christ were to appear today, all of his predictions would have been fulfilled to the letter.

In the next portion of the chapter, Matthew 24:15-25, Jesus speaks especially about the events in connection with the destruction of Jerusalem in A.D. 70. Even verse 21 about the "great distress" (KJV: "great tribulation") can very well be applied to the terrifying events and sufferings of that day. At any rate, it is evident that it does not teach the "Great Tribulation" that the millennarians propose, because verse 22 speaks of the elect as still being on earth during this period of suffering.

The Lord's coming

Jesus describes his coming in Matthew 24:29 and following. He begins by saying, "Immediately after the distress of those days 'the sun will be darkened, and the moon will not give its light; the stars will fall from the sky, and the heavenly bodies will be shaken.' At that time the sign of the Son of Man will appear in the sky, and all the nations of the earth will mourn. They will see the Son of Man coming on the clouds of the sky, with power and great glory." What is "the distress [KJV: "tribulation"] of those days"? Read about it once more in verses 5 to 14. The time of distress, or tribulation, is the entire time of the New Testament. When we have passed through these troubles, we will not enter a millennium but face the last judgment. That we shall also be subjected to these tribulations is clear from the following verse (31), where Christ speaks about what will happen on judgment day: "He will send his angels with a loud trumpet call, and they will gather his elect from the four winds, from one end of the heavens to the other." That, by the way, is the real rapture of the saints, when we go to meet him as he comes in judgment and then stand at his right hand.

That is Jesus' account of the days of the New Testament and his coming again. When we look at it from one angle, they are the years of the millennium. When we look at it from another angle, they are the years of the tribulation. But whether they bring success for the gospel or suffering for the saints, the Lord promises us, "He who stands firm to the end will be saved" (Matthew 24:13). Besides, all these strange and horrible things happening in the world, in human society and in the church, remind us of the Lord's words in Luke 21:28: "When these things begin to take place, stand up and lift up your heads, because your redemption is drawing near."

This is what the Lord teaches. This teaching of his strengthens and consoles us as we pass through this world of trouble. His words let us see not only our troubles but also the Sun of Righteousness. He said, "I am coming soon" (Revelation 22:20). The signs are all there!